WHERE DID MY MONEY GO?

Other books by Jim Jorgensen

The Graying of America
Your Retirement Income
Stay Ahead in the Money Game
How to Make IRAs Work For You
MoneyShock
Money Lessons for a Lifetime
It's Never Too Late to Get Rich

WHERE DID MY MONEY GO?

*A quick lesson in making money in an
Up and Down market*

Jim Jorgensen

iUniverse, Inc.
New York   Bloomington

Where Did My Money Go?
A quick lesson in making money
in an Up and Down market

Copyright © 2008 by Jim Jorgensen

Bull Run Press
Indian Wells, CA
Info@financialsavvy.com
First edition, 2009

iUniverse books may be ordered through
booksellers or by contacting:

iUniverse
1663 Liberty Drive
Bloomington, IN 47403
www.iuniverse.com
1-800-Authors (1-800-288-4677)

ISBN: 978-1-4401-3047-2 (pbk)
ISBN: 978-1-4401-3048-9 (ebk)

Printed in the United States of America

iUniverse rev. date: 3/23/2009

Dedicated to my wife,
Nancy Jorgensen
who taught me everything
I know about life.

Contents

Forward

THE INVESTING WORLD HAS CHANGED
dramatically in the 2000s compared to the roaring
1990s. Investors in the 90s had started to think
that annual 20% gains from Standard & Poor's
500 Index funds were their constitutional right
and that making money in stocks was easy

But the 2000s have been a very different story
indeed. A continuing unfolding of one major
corporate scandal after another has severely
shaken investor confidence in the whole system
of investing. All of the major institutions that
were supposed to protect investors—the corporate
board of directors, auditors, accountants, stock
analysts, investment bankers, stock exchanges,
attorneys general, state and federal securities
regulators—all failed to uncover or stop massive

fraud and shareholder abuse by a laundry list of American corporations including Enron, Adelphia, Global Crossing, Qwest, WorldCom and many, many others.

So what is the investor supposed to do in this new environment—climb under a rock and hide for the rest of the decade? That certainly won't help you fund your retirement nest egg! *In Where Did My Money Go?* Jim Jorgensen says don't hide—adapt to the new reality! Jim has seen these cycles before in his 35 years of advising investors on his nationally syndicated radio shows and seminars. So he doesn't get thrown while many other less seasoned advisors are throwing in the towel and losing all credibility with their clients.

In this era, investors who learn about how to play the markets on their own will do fantastically well, while those who rely on "experts" like brokers and stock analysts will probably end up losing even more money than they did in the Bursting Bubble early 2000s. Jim makes it easy by introducing a simple system to avoid losing money in down markets and a way to profit from a rising markets. This book is quick, enjoyable and an easy read. And if you put its teaching into practice and into your life, you will end up being a far richer, more comfortable investor than the vast majority of Americans who are either still hiding under that proverbial rock or are still trying to play the game like it was in the 1990s!

—Jordan Elliot Goodman, former Wall Street correspondent for Money Magazine, author of Everyone's Money Book.

Chapter 1
Let's Begin

If you invested in the stock market during the past few years you probably feel like Howard Beale in the 1976 film *Network* when he says: "I'm mad as hell, and I'm not going to take it any more."

You're mad because your broker or financial planner told you to buy Enron or Washington Mutual or some computer stock set to double in price because they were making huge profits. You're mad because you later lost your money when the profits turned out to be nothing more than a classic case of cooking the books. You're mad because the rush into mortgage debt was said to be as safe as cash and turned out to be almost worthless. And you're mad because analysts on Wall Street made millions of dollars while they told investors to buy the stocks they privately ridiculed. All the while you were glued to the doom and gloom each day as the stocks and funds continued to slide. You probably felt alone, flying without a safety net. Like a caller on the air told me, "the stock market shock feels like a guy in a bath tub holding a toaster – and in this plunging market no one knows when to let go!"

During this period you may also have stuck you head under the covers. And, like many buy-and-hold investors your investment statements have been tucked into a file box unopened. Now, as we face 2009, you can buy a share of Citigroup – the nation's largest bank – that sold for $55 at the beginning of 2007 for $2.50. ATM fees can run that much. Or, for the price of a share of General Motors stock, you can buy a spark plug. Or for less than the price of a toaster you can buy a share of General Electric stock. You probably no longer feel like a bull. You may, in fact, have become an ostrich.

What the recent stock market meltdown has once again told us is that a sick in the sand approach to investing is guaranteed to lose most of your past gains. In fact, the Ostrich effect is the reason most people sit on their hands and end up with only a modest retirement account.

Everyone wants to do something, but fear erupts and rational thoughts go out the window. But is fear and denial the best way to manage your financial future? Not if you want to build a retirement nest egg for your retirement years. In fact, this book is about ways to encourage you to make a commitment to change the way you invest in the future.

Like most investors, in this prolonged period of a crashing and soaring stock market, you probably avoided making any changes in the way you manage money. Instead, you're waiting for the stocks or mutual funds to regain their value. History tells us, however, when you stand pat things could get worse and they usually do.

As you survey the smoking wreckage of your IRA and 401(k), you probably wonder: *What should I do now?* The answer is to remember that most of the people frozen in fear and standing pat didn't realize how their funds were hammered over the preceding three and five years. Take some of the largest stock funds, like the $28.6 billion Magellan fund. Buy-and-hold investors lost 46 percent of their nest egg for the year ending in October 2008, and for the past three years the fund lost 26 percent. Or take the big Value fund, down almost 41 percent for this same period and down 24 percent over the past three years. Here's why:

The secret to prosperity is your ability and desire to adopt changes in the way you manage your money.

But if the market turmoil hasn't frightened you, if you're not ready to take charge of your own investments, then I want to share some of my experience in investing.

The secret of building a nest egg today is making money in an up market and avoid losing that same money in a down market.

Time magazine's January 28, 2002, issue told investors: "With so many choices and no one to trust in today's world, *you're on your own, baby.*"

The article asked: "Can I count on my broker? Who's looking after my 401(K)?" *Time* concluded that the old safety nets are gone. And it really is true: You're on your own baby!

But if you can change what you *believe,* you can change what *you do.* As a result, the first thing you need to believe is that like *Time* magazine you're on your own and you can successfully management your money. I'm not going to claim to know everything about investing – I only know what has worked for me (and what hasn't) over the years. A wise man once said, "If you want to know how you feel about someone, talk about their youth." So let me tell you a little about mine.

I was born in Omaha, Nebraska (along with Warren Buffett) and grew up in a household that today would be called economically disadvantaged. I didn't know that at the time, but I did know since my family did not own a car, that if I wanted to go someplace I walked. And when I went to a birthday party I had to bring a gift. My mom usually bought the gift, but one day she gave me a dollar to buy one. "What can I buy?" I asked. She said, "Buy whatever you'd like, I'm sure Johnny will like it, too." I went to the store and found just what I'd always wanted. All I had to do was convince my mom to let me keep it. I tried the ploy that Johnny might not like it and maybe we should get another gift. Mom didn't buy that. Then I said it had batteries and maybe we should open the' package to make sure they were still good. Mom said we'd trust the batteries. I even tried to get sick the day of the birthday party in the hope that Mom would forget about the gift.

Do you know what it's like to give a birthday gift that you've always wanted to someone else? That's the whole deal with birthday parties, except I never forgot that day and I vowed that someday I'd learn how to make enough money in the stock market to buy the things I wanted.

Later in life my family moved to a small farming town of maybe 800 people in California. I learned my first basic money management lessons in high school when I visited my dad, who was an accountant at a farm machinery store. I can still remember pulling five-cent Cokes from a tub of cold water and talking with the farmers. They wore bib overalls and talked about the new tractors, the hay rakes, and about money. At first appearance these farmers didn't appear to be sophisticated money managers, but they always, drove big Cadillac's and knew the value of a dollar saved.

When I went to the university I discovered that business professors never talked to the farmers, never drove Cadillacs, and saved only a few dollars a month instead of creating investment portfolios. Maybe that's why none of them taught courses on getting rich. I learned how to accomplish that from the farmers.

What I've tried to incorporate in this book is the difference between people who actively manage their money and those who don't. Those who make money in up markets and don't lose the same money in down markets. The importance of this plan became clear, even to those who never look at their mutual fund statements, when the stock market wiped out 40, even 50 percent of their retirement nest egg in 2008.

I gave early pre-publication copies of this book to my employees and to those who listened to my radio show because I was eager to explain ways to bring success in their financial lives and, for the first time, imagine themselves managing their own money.

Money is often the soul of our well-being. We pursue it each workday because we believe it will make us happy. But if we get it and then lose it, we can face a traumatic future. If we get it, keep it and make it grow, it can lead us to a full and rewarding life with the people we love.

Over the years I've learned that the most

important things you can do in life are to make yourself happy, to share your love and understanding with your family, and to take each day one day at a time. After all, your trip to financial success should be as much fun as arriving at the destination.

What I've learned over 30-years in the financial markets is what you'll read in this book. It's also my belief that if you follow the 15-minute a week plan in Trend Investing it can literally be the difference between retiring rich and working behind a fast-food counter.

I hope each time you read this book you'll find something new and useful for yourself, you're loved ones and your friends. I'm glad that I can share what I've learned and I wish you well as you build your financial future.

Chapter 2
Stuck in the Same Rut

On a Saturday morning at Starbucks, as was my custom, I had coffee with the gang. We talked about last week's golf game and about how many of our friends were losing money in the stock market.

"Look at me," a guy in workout gym clothes said. "I've worked for the same company for fifteen years and after socking all that money into my 401(k) and IRAs, they're not worth much more than the money I invested."

"I hear you," another said, "but each Saturday we've been having coffee you've been telling me the same story. You can't deny what's been happening and then do nothing but complain. You're just stuck in the same rut."

"I know," he said, laying his newspaper on the table. "I've done what I've always done. I invested my money each month and each year the overall balance inches up if it moves at all.   But this last year, with the stock market meltdown, it feels like I'm dropping dollar bills in front of my lawn mower."

The problem, I explained to my friends, is that everyone has to cope with unexpected changes. It can make life complicated and challenging, but if you resist change because it's new or unfamiliar you can be taken by surprise and find out that most of what you want out of life is no longer within reach.

That's because, sooner or later, you're going to have to understand that if you want to invest in individual stocks or mutual funds you'll have to find someone to look after your money. That someone might not be a fund salesperson disguised as a financial planner, not an investment advisor at the bank, not a local friend.

Today that someone is you!

In fact, the chances are you may have depended on others without realizing that no one really cares about your money as much as you do. Ask yourself - did any one call you on your sinking mutual funds? Did you learn about the plummeting Washington Mutual, Lehman Brothers and Citicorp stock?

You may also realize, with your hands off approach, you no longer leap for the letter opener when your investment statements arrive. You seldom look up the value of your portfolio. What was once a vague sense of fear about the future has transformed itself into unmistakable terror that your financial world could collapse at any time.

When you look over your mutual fund statements, what kind of mood are you in? What do you *want* to see in those statements? Do you sense that you are torn between letting things go to the next statement just to see if things get better, or pick up the phone and try to *do* something?

Maybe you're stuck in a comfortable rut that you've followed for years. I like to think it's like wearing old shoes. After my feet get comfortable in a pair of shoes, I keep them until they fall apart. As long as they feel and look good, why throw them away? This drives my wife nuts. But for many investors, keeping old comfortable shoes is a lot like keeping old comfortable stocks and mutual funds. As long as things haven't fallen completely apart, why make a change?

The cruel fact is that only when you have the desire, and especially the confidence to make changes in the way you invest, will you make money in the stock market.

Chapter 3
The Turtle and The Hare

Let me tell you a common fable about the Turtle and the Hare.

The Turtle was an investor who worked hard, earned a modest living and had pieced together a small nest egg. The Hare was a Wall Street broker who lived in a million-dollar pad. With option and trading bonuses, the fast-moving Hare made over a million a year. For the Hare, the race was already over; his hefty nest egg was in the bank.

The hundred grand the Turtle had saved was all he had and it was his retirement security. But the income the Hare could make on this kind of money was not worth returning phone calls. In the fee-based brokerage world the Hare needed individual accounts of at least a quarter million to make the working arrangement with clients pay.

Nevertheless, the Turtle expected the fast moving Hare, who had one eye on Wall Street and one eye on the trading floor, to look after his investments. When the Hare finally called and said the bulls were running again the Turtle took his advice and waited for the hand-picked stocks and mutual funds he was offered to prosper. Instead, in an orgy of flame outs and crashes, the especially selected stocks and funds plunged in value.

Alone in the fast changing financial world, the Turtle became concerned about the shrinking value of his investment. He called the fast-moving Hare. He was told that while his investments were sinking, not to worry. The firm's New York security analysts continued to have a *buy* recommendation on these stocks and mutual funds. One stock, he was told, was expected to have a target price at least $20 above its current $40 price.

The Turtle had to discover on his own that the broker's New York buy recommendation had never rebounded and the stock is now trading for $5 a share. For a slow moving Turtle, who had built a nest egg on hard work and savings, this was scary stuff indeed. He finally understood that his fear of managing his own money had held him – and his money – captive by the Hare.

The fast-moving Hare quickly moved on to sniff out bigger piles of cash, while the slow-moving Turtle was left to remember that most of what he once had was gone.

The important lesson for the Turtle was:

When he was sitting on his hands bleeding to death no one was interested in his stocks and funds.

Chapter 4
The 15 Minute Manager

The 15-minute a week manager is based on Trend Investing. This is ultimately a story about gaining the ability to protect your investments in a falling market and using the cash to later buy back your stocks to double your money in an up market. Make no mistake, to be a successful Trend Investor you have to have the guts and determination to quickly buy and sell your securities.

The problem is that most people understand buying a stock or mutual fund is much easier than selling one. To buy you only need the basic optimism that the stock will go up and create wealth. To sell you have to admit you were wrong. That's hard for many people to do.

But if it's a loss or a gain, you have to act like a cold-blooded vampire because a mutual fund is not going to call you and tell you its fund is going into the tank. Nor is it likely that a broker or financial planner will pick up the phone and give you the bad news. In fact, the chances are no one is going to call you. As *Time* magazine tells us, we're in a world of do-it-yourself investing. **You're on your own baby!**

Managing my money myself I look at the original investment as the starting point. As the months unfold I'm willing to lock in a profit even if the price goes higher later on. That's because, once the stock price trends downward you can't live on hope that it will rebound.

Here's how the 15-minutes a week Trend Investing works:

The first step:

Buy the Saturday *New York Times, Wall Street Journal* or other paper with the stock and fund tables. As you move to the web, you can replace the papers with www.bigcharts.com. Simply type the stock or fund's ticker symbol and you'll have a current and 1-3-5 year stock price history.

You can also list your stocks and funds on your brokerage web site. This page will automatically keep track of your stocks and funds each time you go to the web site.

The second step:

Check the value of your investments – the stocks and mutual funds in your personal account, your IRA, 401(k) or 403(b) each week. For many years a group of us did this each Saturday morning at Starbucks and reviewed the end of the week numbers. But, remember it's not the recent golf game; it's the numbers you're after. Then keep a log of each security, its purchase price, current price and price trend.   That's because, as you already know:

The mutual fund is not going to call and tell you the fund is going into the tank. Nor is it likely your investment adviser will tell you the bad news. In fact, for most investors, no one is going to call.

The third step:

Now you know where you stand. If the stock or fund has fallen more than 5 percent from its recent high, or 5 percent under your original purchase price, sell. If you read where the Dow Jones Industrial Averages took a big hit, you might want to check your holdings and sell mid-week. If you feel the stock or fund is in a forced sharp decline, you may want to sell immediately.

I promise you'll feel a sense of relief as you watch other investors, who continued to hang on in the eternal belief that in a plunging stock market the price will come roaring back, continue to lose money.

Again, the important point: When your stocks or mutual funds are down 5 percent from their recent highs or 5 percent from the purchase price just force your self to sell. Don't wait and try to second guess the market. Most of the small investors I've known have gone to the poor house expecting the stock market to run in their favor if they just waited long enough.

Once you get the hang of managing your investments each week you can probably cut the loss on your stock and sell with less than a 5 percent dip in price, but you have to be careful of false bottoms.

The fourth step:

Put the money from the sale of your securities in your money-market or cash account. I call this holding place **The Lock Box.** This is one of the most important steps. It lets you sell at the start of a down market, hold the cash, buy in the up market, and sell again when the stock begins another down trend.

The good news is that it's not very difficult to mange your money if you have a small portfolio of Blue Chip stocks and a few mutual funds. Just 15-minutes a week or less can often cut your losses and keep most of hard-earned money safe. You won't be able to buy and sell at just the right time, nor do you have to. And it's rarely worth spending an additional 90 percent of your time to get a 1 percent increase in performance.

But over time you'll find as I have, you can sharply cut your losses in a down market and use that same money to make big profits in an up market. After all, that's what Wall Street is all about.

Chapter 5
Let's Do The Numbers

Managing your money can be a new game and it can often be a numbers game. And the numbers start as soon as you invest.

But, as you'll find out, the numbers go against the stand patters who can lose two ways even if they later break even.

Let's say you had $20,000 in a mutual fund, but when you got your last statement the fund was worth only $10,000. Your palms are clammy and your heart is pounding as you look at your last statement and think about the hair- raising dive in the market.

If you lose 50 percent of your money and you want to break even, you'll have to make a 100 percent return on what you have left.

What's really running through your mind is how to save what's left of your nest egg. In fact, you probably don't care if you make any money; all you want now is to break even.

But if you lost 50 percent of your money and want to break even, you'll have to make a 100 percent next year on what you have left. As far as I know there aren't many super funds or stocks that can deliver that kind of performance any time soon.

And I've got more bad news you're not going to like. Let's look at making the money back. If you could earn 9 percent a year on the money you lost and avoid paying taxes and other fees, it could take you 8 years to re-build your loss of $10,000 back to $20,000.

But if you avoided the loss in the first place with the 15- minute a week drill, and earned 9 percent each year for 8 years on the money, your mutual fund investment could now total about $40,000 instead of $20,000.

In this case you lost twice!

- When the value of the fund was cut in half.
- When you failed to make any money on the money you lost.

What's different today is that those who stand pat never expected to experience a stomach-churning, crashing and soaring stock market where in one day a stock can lose 20 percent of its price. In fact, never before have some of America's best companies taken investors to the cleaners.

Take this quiz.

Which would you rather do for the next two years?
- (a) Invest in a mutual fund with an 80 percent return one year and a 50 percent loss the next.
- (b) Invest is a 5 percent insured savings account.

My guess is you'd pick the fund that made an 80 percent return, and say, *"let's go for it!"*

But, my friend, you're looking at the screaming headline for a mutual fund with a huge loss the previous year.

Investors can lose more money when share prices fall than they make when share prices rise.

Here's how this works:

With a $10,000 investment in a stock or fund that's earning 80 percent return the first year, you'd have an account balance of $18,000. But with a 50 percent loss in the second year, the account balance falls to $9,000.

With the same $10,000 investment in a 5 percent savings account, the total of the account at the end of two years could be over $11,000.

Now be honest. If you picked the high-flying mutual fund you never thought it could cost you more than you would earn in a laid back savings account. Right? Of course not.

But then you probably believed with an 80 percent gain this was just the fund to make money and not follow the last high-flyer you watched go into the dumpster.

It's what you make over time that's important.

With this example, you won't be better off in

the next 5 years. Let's say the fund continues to return 9 percent a year. At the end of 5 years the savings account, earning 5 percent, could total more than $14,000, while the mutual fund's account could only total about $13,800.

That empty feeling of losing money may have happened to you often in the past, but I know someone who has an answer: Warren Buffett, the most famous investor in America. He puts first things first.

Rule Number 1: *Don't Lose Money*.
When someone asked him what was Rule Number 2, Buffett simply said,
Rule Number 2: *Don't forget Rule number 1*

Sometime we can't see the obvious because we can't see the future from where we stand in the present. Just think of the hard-earned money you've lost in the market that won't be there when you retire. Then think about the money you could have made on the money you lost over the last twenty years.

Let's be honest, Warren Buffett is on to something when he says don't lose money in the market. In fact, I believe this is the really big factor in building your future financial life.

You only have to look at 2008 to see how Buffett's rule comes into play. According to Lipper, who has been tracking stock mutual fund performance records since 1959, if you had $100,000 in your 401(k) plan at the start of that year, you've lost $40,000 by the end of the year.

But the full effect of Buffett's rule becomes clear when you consider you'll have to earn a 66 percent return in the next year on your new balance of $60,000 just to get your account back to where it was a year earlier. What if you can't beat the experts on the Street and earn 66 percent on your 401(k) assets in one year? If you can earn an average annual return of 9 percent you'll need an additional 6 years to turn the $60,000 back into $100,000. Another painful lesson for buy-and-hold investors is that under this example you just lost 6 years of earning a return on your original 401(k) money.

Let's use the $40,000 loss in his example and say you have about 25 years until you collect Social Security. You're probably wondering what it costs to lose this money because you sat on your hands and were afraid to do anything. If you can earn an average 9 percent annual return until you collect Social Security, the money you lost could amount to about a cool $350,000 when you hit retirement age.

The scary part is that, on average each year over that 25-year period, your average annual return on that initial $40,000 you lost could be $14,000 a year! As I was told on the floor of the New York Stock Exchange, an average annual return of 35 percent can make you rich!

Let me explain it this way. Every dollar you lose in the market this year could be ten dollars you won't have at retirement. That's why I say on radio and television if you have any money to invest, no matter how much or how little, this compounding principle can still work for you. Here's why....

80 to 90 percent of the money that ends up in your retirement nest egg could be money you never saved or invested in the first place.

But the clincher might be how much you actually earn on the money you've invested. No one talks about this, but it's the secret of becoming rich.

There's a simple way to determine how fast your money can accumulate and make you rich. It's called the Rule of 72. This rule lets you determine approximately how many years it will take an investment to double in value if the rate or return remains the same.

For example, if you earn an annual 10 percent return, divide 72 into 10 percent. You should be able to double your money in 7.2 years. But with a 5 percent savings account, you'd have to wait almost 15 years just to double your money. And with a 3 percent insured CD, you could wait 24 years to double your money.

Over time these numbers add up.

Suppose you start with $10,000

- A 3 percent annual return over 25 years could grow to about $18,000.
- A 5 percent annual return over 25 years could grow to about $32,250.
- A 10 percent annual return over the same period might total $100,000.
- A 15 percent annual return could be worth about $325,000.

Now you might not earn 15 percent a year in common stocks and funds, but staying in savings accounts at a lower annual rate of return can make a huge difference in your nest egg at retirement.

Fortunately for me and my kids, the lighting bolt hit home when I discovered that I might be able to double my money every 7 years in the stock market, compared to about every 15 years in a fixed savings account.

But, for the first time, let me show you again the effects of a low return over time on building a retirement nest egg.

A one-time deposit of $10,000.

	15-yrs	30-yrs
Savings 5%	$20,000	$43,000
Stocks 10%	$41,700	$175,000

Look at this way. Once you know the rule of 72 you begin to understand how important the percentage of your annual return over time can be. As I've said, the other important point is the magic of compounding, with only a few dollars a day you can build a sizeable retirement nest egg.

The one Latte a day retirement plan

Most people are surprised to learn that regular investing with compounding can build wealth without a lot of money.

Suppose, on your way to work, you pass up the coffee shop and instead invest $5 each work day in your one and only IRA and you manage your money so that you earn a 9 percent average annual return. If you start when you're 30, by age 65 you could have as much as $300,000 in your IRA. With the 15-minute a week drill maybe half a million or more. That can be done if you keep your money in the up markets, and later buy on the dips with Trend Investing.

Sometime we can't see the obvious because we can't see the future from where we stand in the present. You may not have learned the importance of compounding and rate of return in school, but these basic building blocks are the key to becoming rich with only a few dollars a week.

Chapter 6
Building a plan for investing

You may remember the market crash of 1987, or, the market closing after the 9/11 attack. Or the mortgage crisis of 2008. And then in 2009, the worst recession in decades, that sent the stock indexes to their lowest level 12 years.

While buy-and-hold investors watched their holdings take a dive and lose a big part of their nest egg, others were taking advantage of the sharp fall off to buy and later profiting handsomely from the 15-minute weekly drill. In each case, when panic swept the stock market, it was a time to use Trend Investing and the cash in the **Lock Box** and buy good stocks that had fallen to historical lows.

On the other hand, if you continue to believe buy-and-hold can work over time you haven't read the 2007 Lipper Research Study. It found that the total returns over the past 10 years, not counting dividends and inflation, for the Standard and Poor's 500 stock index, was 33 percent, or an average annual return of just 3.3 percent. The Study also pointed out that the Lipper Large-Company Core Index, the fund index most comparable to the S&P 500, gained even less - Just 26 percent over the past ten years, or 2.6 percent a year.

Lipper also found more grim news for buy-and-hold investors. If they had invested $100 a month in the largest stock mutual funds, typically the kind offered in 401(k) plans, their investments tanked.

The average growth and value of the top 10 stock funds, as of October, 2008:
- Over 5 years, total investment $6,000, average market value of funds, $5,850.
- Over 10 years, total investment $12,000, average market value of funds $15,070

Other reports I've read about managing your money say you should not pay $200 a year for an investment advisory newsletter, or grab the 100 best stocks for just five bucks a week. According to Mark Hulbert, who tracks over 100 investment newsletter performances in The Hulbert Financial Digest, only a relatively few actually do better than the overall market.   Or, as I learned on Wall Street, about the same results could be had picking stocks by throwing darts at the wall.   In fact, the Wall Street Journal once had a weekly contest between several stock pickers from major brokerage firms and a staffer throwing darts at the paper's stock pages tacked up on the wall. Flinging the darts won most of the contests. "It was," a friend told me, "too embarrassing to compete with darts," and he agreed that the newspaper should drop the contest.

So you don't need to invest in stocks or funds where the portfolio manager wants you to believe he or she can outguess the stock market. Why? Peter Lynch, who set performance records year after year when he was the portfolio manger for Fidelity's Magellan fund, says trying to time the market is a waste of time. "I don't know anyone who has been right more than once in a row."

It's also a good idea to keep your investment

portfolio simple. Don't let a broker or financial planner design an investment plan that loads you up with several mutual funds and dozens of stocks of highly recommended picks that come with glowing recommendations from Wall Street analysts. You know the kind where you find out later that the *buy* recommendation wasn't a sure thing, and the *hold* should have been *sell*.

If you have $10,000 to invest, you could have maybe five stocks. With $50,000 or more, your portfolio could include ten stocks. Like Warren Buffett, it's better to invest in just a few stocks you know well and understand the industry so you can pull the 15 - minute drill each Saturday, than play the whole market and be overwhelmed keeping track of what's going on.

But with only a few stocks you've got to be choosy and invest only in the bluest of blue chips. The thirty stocks that make up the Dow Jones Industrial Averages are usually some of the biggest names in America and owned by more investors than almost any other stock. In fact, I learned on Wall Street that the more investors who own a stock the more likely you are to make money on that stock.

The good news is that you don't have to be a financial wizard to succeed like Warren Buffett.

You just need to understand the basics of investing and managing your money that came from growing up poor. As a bonus, following these rules could even earn you a little cocktail *braggadocio* over your earnings.

Here are the important points for building a nest egg:

First you have to make sure you've invested in the right stocks.

Invest in a company that's been profitable

The company must have reported strong earnings over a period of at least five years. It has more cash than long-term debt, and its profit margins are at or above the industry standards. Ideally, earnings growth should be accelerating from one quarter to the next, or increase at least 20 percent a year for the last three years.   Unprofitable companies or start ups do occasionally rocket up the charts, but don't bet on them.

Remember, for the most part, the price of a stock will follow its earning per share. In fact, if you lay a chart of the price of the stock over the past few years on top of a chart of the earnings per share, the lines will typically mirror each other.

Earnings are also important when the stock market takes a dive. In those cases, the stocks with good earnings will typically fare better. As they say on Wall Street: A company that isn't making money for itself can't make money for investors.

Don't invest in retail and consumer products

Avoid investing in companies that sell products through department stores, discount stores, grocery stores, or have retail stores. These historically have been poor performers. The companies face two problems: One, they have to wait for the consumer to come in the front door, and two, they face new competition almost every day.

Like grocery stores from Costco and Wal-Mart, electronic stores like Best Buy from the furniture stores who offer large size television sets below their prices.

Never invest in a regulated industry

Forget about energy companies, telephone companies and airlines. These companies are often limited by regulations to what they can charge for their services. If they can't make a lot of money you don't want to own the stock.

Invest in a long time market leader

You want a well-established company with a strong customer demand for its product and therefore a clear lock on the market. It could be a unique product like Coca-Cola, or branches on every corner like Bank of America.

Invest in a well-known brand name

The reason is that corporate brand familiarity helps attract buyers of the stock. A study by Corporate Branding LLC, a brand-strategy consultant, found that in a ten year study of thirty-two companies those found to have the strongest brands had a return of 402 percent, compared with 309 percent for the Dow Jones Industrial Averages.

Invest in a company at least twenty years old

It takes at least twenty years for a company to establish itself and have a solid enough position in the industry to assure continued profits and growth. If you feel compelled to chase the latest hot stock, consider what happened to investors in the last start up collapse.

From these painful reminders you can learn that it's better to come to the party late, or not at all.

Never buy a cheap stock

Its human nature to think that a stock you've been considering buying for sometime is now a bargain after its shares have plunged to new lows.

You're told the traffic light has tuned from red to amber, and it's just the right time to step on the gas. But after a stock has taken a big dive the chances are the big institutional traders and mutual fund managers have probably already slammed on the brakes. That leaves the individual investors seeking a low price stock headed for a big-time crash.

Never invest in companies with a share price below $10.

If the stock market has a remainder bin, it's reserved for those stocks under $10. Wall Street derisively refers to these socks as *single-digit midgets.* In fact, once the share price falls below $5 a share the fat lady has already sung and the party is over. Typically, the stock will fall off Wall Street's radar and be known as *penny stocks.*

Next, we'll find out when to buy and sell the stocks and funds.

Chapter 7
Trend Investing

I suggest the following approach to Trend Investing:

Rule 1: Invest in hot companies

Rule 2: Sell as soon as they turn cold

To accomplish these tasks Trend Investing requires you to not only recognize the start of an upward trend and a downward trend, but the recovery of the upward trend. In order to do this it's important to understand that **you are not picking stocks in the classic way.**

This strategy saves a lot of time since you don't have to read about the hot stock picks or focus on operating margins, debt levels, and capital expenditures to identify the best investments.

Scores of books have been written on the value strategy and how to look for stocks selling at an attractive price. You are not a bargain hunter. You're not interest if management has an excellent track record or the firm's return on equity. You're not looking for a fundamental analysis of earnings per share or the size of the dividend payout. You are also not a financial newsletter reader who learns about stocks you should already have sold. Instead, you are simply reading the newspaper looking for industries or sectors with a strong demand for the product or services that you think will continue to grow or decline. Like oil companies when gas was $3 a gallon headed over $4, when home builders could not meet the demand for new home sales, and when customers reduced their daily trips to the coffee shops.

Need ideas for picking your next stock? Why not take a trip to the local shopping mall and see what's new and popular? As you read the paper study what new products have been introduced, what businesses are going to be affected by the economy, what new product you think will take off. You are looking for the introduction of a new product like pantyhose that swept the competitors off the department store shelves. One of my best finds was Hansen Natural, a soft drink maker who discovered the health foods market, and then launched the number two energy drink Monster.

Consider each item of interest a potential investing idea. Find out from the packaging the name of the manufacturer, then race to Google to see if the stock is listed and its history. You will know you are on to something when you find your friends want to buy one of the product or services you've discovered.

Then find a company who is a leader in the industry. If you invest in a well-known company it's unlikely you'll wake up in a cold sweat when the company stock has taken a nose dive or bankruptcy is on the horizon. Companies like Coca Cola, General Electric, Wal-Mart, American Express and DuPont will be here a long time.

Once you've spotted the industry trend do your 15-minute a week drill. Watch the company stock. If you're right, and the industry is **hot**, you should see an increase in expected earnings and a spike in the price of the stock.

Once the stock is up 5 percent from the recent low, buy! This should confirm an upward trend.

Again, reading the newspapers you began to

see signs of a cooling in the industry. Sales are slowing down, problems are developing and stories have appeared of possible problems in the future. Each week review your price logs and when the stock has declined 5 percent from its high, sell. After you sell the price of the stock could always bounce higher, but as they say on Wall Street: "It's better to leave some on the table than end up with too little to eat."

Take the home builders. In 2006 home buyers lined up at the new developments eager to buy a new home at almost any price. With profits rolling in, home builder's stock was on a sharp upswing. The industry was **Hot**.

But the mortgage meltdown put a lot of homes on the market and real estate values plunged. Builders no longer built homes they could not sell. The industry turned **cold.**

A trip to Starbucks

But with Trend Investing you might also start in reverse with an industry starting to turn **cold** and wait for it to turn **hot.**

At the start of 2008 I held 100 shares of Starbuck stock at $35 a share. But as the economy went into a deeper slump and jobs were disappearing at a fast pace, I read where people were backing off buying Starbuck lattés at $4 plus. I visited the local stores, talked to the staff, and I learned the news reports were true. Thinking sales would continue to decline and profits would take a major hit as people avoided the pricey coffee, I sold the stock after a 5 percent decline at $33.25 a share.

Again, the stock could always take a leap upward after I sold, but as I've said, it's better to leave some money on the table. Anyway, I put $3,325 into my cash **Lock Box.**

Watching the stock each week I found that I was right. By October 2008, with the slowdown at the coffee counter, the stock had fallen to just $10.50 a share. But I stayed on the sidelines, the economy wasn't getting any better and my visit to the coffee shop told me that business had again slowed and the shares had fallen to $9.60. That was good enough for me. With the money in the **Lock Box** from the recent sale of Starbuck stock, I was in a perfect position to buy back the stock. I converted the cash into 346 shares of stock. My original investment was the same, only the number of shares I owned had changed.

But when the economy recovers and people return to their habit of rushing back into the coffee shops, I will be one happy guy. Starbuck stock could at least return to 75 percent of its former price, or $26.25 a share. Now I'm the chips, making money like walking the floor of the New York Stock Exchange.   Instead of an account worth $2,625 on 100 shares holding onto the stock, I could have $9,082 on 346 shares – all because of Trend Investing.

Sitting on the sidelines and the 15 minute weekly drill with Trend Investing it turns out can really pay off!

Chapter 8
Never give up on a stock

The next lesson is another example of Trend Investing.

Suppose we start with a make-believe company called ABC. Although it's a solid company, because of market and economic conditions and antitrust concerns the price of ABC stock begins the year at $100 a share as demand for its product soars. Then economic conditions later result in a downturn and the stock falls to $50 in May. Then, when the entire market takes off, the stock rebounds to $100 a share by the end of December. For the buy-and-hold investor the return on his 100 shares of ABC stock for the year is zero, along with a few sleepless nights. But if the investor follows the 15-minute a week drill and sells when the stock is down 5 percent, or $95 a share, keeps the money in the **Lock Box**, and buys back the stock at mid-year at $52.50 a share after a 5 percent upturn, the trend investor can buy 181 shares of ABC stock.

But here's what's wonderfully easy to understand.   At the end of the year the buy-and-hold investor has 100 shares @ $100 a share, or $10,000. But the trend investor, with the same amount of money originally invested, has 181 shares, or $18,100. As I've said before, my friend, that's the key to the way I invest. As the stock market climbs the Trend investor's 181 shares of ABC will return a huge advantage over the stand patter's one hundred. How big an advantage? If ABC Shares rise $15 a share the Trend Investor gains $2,715, the buy-and-hold only $1,500.

Of course, Trend Investing doesn't work perfectly every time, and this example of selling and buying ABC stock does not reflect the fact that the price of the stock can plunge and soar several times within one year. But the primary method used in this plan has never completely failed me.

Here are some examples of recent investments using the 15 – minute weekly drill:

KB Homes

I bought stock in the nation's largest home builder - KB Homes - when the housing boom was underway and builders could not build new homes fast enough to avoid a buyer's bidding war.

I sold near the top of the market when listings for selling homes began to pile up at the real estate offices and builders had tracts of unsold homes. By selling in January instead of waiting until the end of the year, I captured my gains rather than holding them and let the market wipe out most of my profits.

Then, when the stock was 5 percent off what I believed was the bottom in Nov, 2008 @ $12 a share. I used the $32,000 cash in the **Lock Box** to buy back the stock.

Here's a review of K B Homes:
October, 2004 buy 400 shares @ $30 $12,000
January, 2006 sell 400 shares @ $80 $32,000
Nov, 2008 buy 2,666 shares @ $ 12 $32,000

The important points are:
- I still have $12,000 invested in the stock from my original purchase.
- I now have 2,666 shares instead of 400 shares

Once the housing industry comes back and home builders again have eager buyers the stock could be 50 percent off its previous high, or $40 a share. My account could then be worth $106,640 vs. buy-and-hold of $16,000.

ExxonMobil

Oil and Gas was another good example of a *hot* sector turning *cold.* When the price of oil skyrocketed to over $3 a gallon at the pump I knew I was right in investing in ExxonMobil. Every time I gassed up my car I smiled at the money I was making on the stock.

But in January, 2008, as the price of a gallon of gas soared over $4 and the problems doubled in the Middle East, I figured the industry was turning *cold.*

Then in October, 2008, when the price of oil dropped from $140 a barrel to $50 a barrel, I went to the **Lock Box** and re-bought the shares. Again, maybe not at the lowest price, but a good turn around level.

Here's a review of ExxonMobil
July, 2006 buy 400 shares @ $60 $ 24,000
January, 2008 sell 400 shares @$88   35,200
October, 2008 buy 541 shares @$65   35,200

Profits so far are $11,200, or a 47 percent return on an original investment of just $24,000.

The good news? I almost doubled my money while other people were bleeding to death at the gas pump.

More good news. With 541 shares, and even a $10 a share increase, I could have $40,575 in my account. A stand patter, with the original 400 shares, I would only have $30,000. Best of all, I'm set to watch the stock head higher with an economic recovery.

Bank of America

In October, 2007 I held 400 shares of Bank of America stock. From reading the papers I could tell that declining home sales and falling prices could put a lot of homeowners at risk dropping the value of the bank's mortgage loan portfolio. I then sold at $55 a share when the sub-prime mortgage mess had begun to affect the bank stocks.

I watched the mortgage mess take the stock down to $ 6 a share by February, 2009. This was a historically low price for this stock. The second largest bank in the country was in good overall condition, but its stock was hit by an entire industry cool down. It was time to re-buy at 5 percent up tick at $6.30 a share.

Here's a review of Bank of America:
October, 2007 sell 400 shares @ $55 $22,000
July, 2008 buy 3,492 shares @$6.30 $22,000

When the economy recovers and the mortgage mess is history, the share price may not return to $55 a share, but the stock could return to half its former high, or $27.50 a share. My 3,492 shares would then be worth $96,030. The buy and hold investor, with the original 400 shares, could have an account worth $11,000.

With a good-quality stock like Bank of America, a solid customer base and branches all over America, and integrating stock broker Merrill Lynch into their branching system, I believe it will prosper in any economic recovery. It is a typical stock that you can watch turn hot, cold, and hot again.

General Electric

The good news is you can follow Trend Investing right along side the money man from Omaha. Maybe you don't have $3 billion in cash lying around the home, but Warren Buffett has. His company, Berkshire Hathaway, put $3 billion into General Electric stock. With the stock selling for $38 a share in April 2008, it had fallen to $24 by October. In this case, Buffett knew the hot stock was turning cold.

Buffett's deal: the right to buy up to $3 billion in GE common stock at $22.25 a share for five years. But to sweeten the play, while he is waiting to buy the stock, the loan to GE pays 10 percent interest each year.

The day he made the deal General Electric's common stock closed at $21.57. Again, Buffett was on to something. One of the nation's largest companies, and one of the 30 Dow stocks, GE shares had just closed at an 11-year low. If Buffett is right, the stock should be back to its recent high of over $38 a share in a couple years. Even without collecting interest, that's a 60% return on the money.

But Trend Investing beat Buffett to his own game. With the 15-minute drill each week I was able to wait until January, 2009 and buy the stock at $12 a share. If the stock closes over $38 a share I can make $26 a share with Trend Investing. That's over a hundred percent return

– numbers they like on the floor of the NYSE and I do in my pocketbook.

In most cases, a buy-and-hold investor will have half the account balance of an investor who sells when the stock goes down and buys back when the stock tends upward.

My motto is never give up on good quality stocks with a solid track record of earnings and a dominate place in the marketplace.

In most cases, if you have a history of buying and selling the company stock, it's an automatic buy if the stock falls to historically low prices when panic strikes the market. In my experience, when everyone wants to bail out of their stocks that's the time to buy. And you'll almost always make money.

Chapter 9
Investing With Time

I can remember when I never looked at my stocks and funds. I didn't think buying and selling made any difference. After all, I reasoned, everyone was doing the same thing so I thought everything would work out in the end. Then I discovered one of the most important factors in building wealth: **Come-Back-Gains with the power of compounding in a rising stock market.**

Let's say, in our previous example of trading Starbuck stock, I sold the stock at $33.25 a share after a 5 percent decline. Based on lower foot traffic into the coffee stores, I later bought back the stock at $ 9.60 a share and converted my money into 346 shares.

At that time the buy-and-hold investor continued to have 100 shares worth $ 960. But in this same example, the Trend Investor could have 346 shares worth $3,321. The difference is an additional $2,361. But this next secret of building wealth is something most people usually don't think about:

How the money you make in the market day by day can affect your ultimate nest egg.

And this type of gain over the buy-and-hold investor can continue for years as the two of them build their retirement nest egg. When you multiply this advantage out for 15 or 20 years the results of compounding the numbers in this one example becomes astounding.

Now let's assume both investors are 40 with 25 years to retirement and sell the Starbuck stock. The buy-and-hold investor still has his or her 100 shares worth $26.25 a share, or $2,625. But the Trend Investor with 346 shares has an account worth $9,082.

If this money is in an IRA, the buy-and-hold

investor's $2,625, earning a 9 percent annual return, could amount to $22,575 at age 65. The Trend Investors' IRA would be worth $ 9,082. With an annual return of 9 percent a year this difference could accumulate to almost $78,105 at age 65. Do this on only a few different stocks and you could have a base for a substantial retirement nest egg.

Another look at the power of compounding

The magic of compounding is that each year your money earned money the entire previous balance in your account, and on any new contributions for that year. The really big secret is that as the years unfold, and the total amount in the account grows, the more you automatically earn each year.

Let's start by putting a penny on your dresser and each night thereafter on your way to bed you double the number of pennies on the dresser top. After ten days, you'd have $5.12. By continuing to double the number of pennies each night, you'd reach $163.84 by the fifteenth night. But in just five more days, you'd need a big dresser top. The pile of pennies would now total $10,485.76. At the twenty-fifth day, the amount would have grown to

$167,772.16.   At the end of just the first thirty days, the pile of pennies will have taken over your bedroom. You now have a total of $5,368,709.12. In just a few more days you'd have every penny in the country on your dresser top.

The 500 Pennies-a-day Program

Now, let's apply the penny saved each day to your retirement savings. You can't double your pennies each day, but assume you can save 500 pennies a day over the next 15-years and you earn a 9 percent annual return. That's a $1,825 yearly IRA contribution. This simple plan, saving 500 pennies a day, could be worth over $100,000 in 20 years.

But here's one secret of compounding. If you can do this for just another 5 years, with a piggy bank in the corner of your room, you've hit the jackpot. Your investment account could then total a whopping $170,000.

No, that's not a misprint. In the period from 20 to 25 years - only an additional five year's contributions of $ 9,125 - the retirement plan could grow from $100,000 to $170,000. That's a hefty $ 70,000 gain. Not bad? Over the last five years, with the power of compounding, you turned $9,100 of contributions into about $70,000.

That, my friend, is an average annual gain of about $14,000 a year with only a $1,825 annual contribution. Turning $1,825 into $14,000 a year is the magic of compounding working for you!

But here's the scary part most people don't realize. If you contribute $1,825 each year for 25 years, that's $45,625. If you have about $170,000 in your IRA at the end of the period, that's a gain of $124,375. Divide that gain by 25 years, compounding provided an average annual buildup of about $5,000 on an annual investment of just $1,825!

If you're unsure when to begin saving for your retirement compounding can make a compelling reason for right now! Consider this: A one-time investment of $10,000 today, earning a 9 percent annual return, by a 30-year old, could amount to about $135,000 at age 65.

Even if you think the stock market won't return to its former levels, assume that you can earn a 7 percent annual return. In that case, the 30-year old could have about $105,000 for a one-time deposit of $10,000.

If you remember nothing else from this book, burn this into your mind: compounding is the most important factor in accumulating money over time

Chapter 10
Retirement plans

Like most investors and retirees you probably have part of your money in IRAs, 401(k)s, 403(b) s and company retirement plans. How can you manage that money if all I talk about is trading stocks?

Managing IRAs

For the most part, using Trend Investing, I manage the money outside and inside my IRA the same way. The only difference is that you can't deduct the losses inside an IRA, which make selling in a down market very important, but you can defer income taxes on the stock trades until you take out the money.

But the big problem I hear on the air is how to manage an IRA. A typical caller asks:

"I've got stuff in my IRA that's been there for some time and hasn't gone anywhere. You talk about change, but I can't figure out what to do with these turkeys."

"That's easy," I replied. "Each IRA has a trustee so the IRS knows when you make a taxable withdrawal. The trustee also typically holds the securities in the account and sends you the statements. To make a change all you have to do is find another investment firm you like. With your permission, they can get the money from your current IRA trustee and transfer it to your new IRA. You can do this as often as you like and this is not a taxable event."

"It's that easy to change my IRA?" the caller exclaimed.

"Absolutely," I said. "But don't worry; you can have as many IRAs as you want, you're just limited by the annual contribution limit."

For example, you can set up an IRA and follow the 15–minute a week drill, buy and sell stocks and funds and automatically roll the money into and out of the **Lock Box**.

Managing employer retirement plans

The hard part for most investors is managing the 401(k), 403(b), or other company plans. For many workers it's often like holding a leaking watering can where the money from their paycheck goes in the top and drains out the bottom while they feel like they're stuck in lead shoes nailed to the floor.

And while your mutual funds are going no place inside a company retirement plan believe me almost no one is going to help you manage your money. That may be why the majority of people I've talked with on the air never look at their mutual funds, or learn how their employer retirement plan works. But if you don't know your options to make changes and smart ways to manage your money you can be committed to a wild ride off into the future. A future where you either take charge of your investments or continue to watch those funds you never touch sink in value.

The reason? Most employer plans typically offer selected mutual funds from a family of funds and it can be difficult to change fund options inside the plan.

The solution? Understand your options for change and that over the past few years the typical growth stock fund has loaded up on the new generation of internet, telecom and mortgage debt that the gorillas on Wall Street though would blast off into outer space. Instead, for many investors, these funds came back to earth in a crash. For employees who ignored their mutual funds the market bust has turned their retirement accounts into disaster zones and a big chunk of their previous value has vanished.

I hear that from people who say it can be hell to watch the stock market take the value of their retirement account down the tubes and they can't figure how to stop the losses. Let's find out.

Grab the SPD

When you became a participant in your employer's plan, or when you asked for one, you should receive a copy of the **Summary Plan Description – SPD.** This booklet explains how your employer plan benefits become vested, how service and benefits are calculated, when you will begin to receive benefits, how to file for payouts and when you can change your investment options.

Effective in 2007, the new Pension Protection Act required Plan Administrators to provide a benefit statement at least once a quarter to participants in plans in which they can self-direct their accounts, and at least once a year to participants in plans in which they cannot self-direct the investments and upon request to any beneficiary.

Your opportunity to change investments inside your company retirement plan could come once a month, once a quarter or once every six months. Some of the newer plans will even let you change investments on line.

Once you are permitted to make a change, find the performance of your current mutual funds. Simply go to www.bigcharts.com and type in the name of the fund. This should give you the ticker symbol. Type that in and you can see the current-1-2-3-4-and 5 year track record. You will see a graph of the share price for each month and you have a quick grasp of the fund's performance. I suggest you do this as part of your 15-minute weekly drill. Again, when you see the share price decline more than 5 percent in a down market, find out from your plan administrator how you can sell and move into a cash account.

After that, each time you have the option to change mutual fund selections, rebalance your account. It's like investing in stocks. If the fund's share price falls 5 percent or more from its high sell the fund and go into cash. At least that will stop the bleeding.

For a new mutual fund selection, I suggest you pick the best equity, stock or stock index fund in the family of funds you are offered. Again, check the current fund's past performance on Bigcharts.com.

Job hopping a new way of life

Another problem is what to do with the money in your employer's retirement plan when you change jobs. The simple answer: roll over your company retirement plan assets to a new IRA you've established for that purpose. You can again set up an IRA as a stock trading account and manage your money every week. If you keep the rollover IRA separate, you can later roll over the money into a new employer's plan. Or, if the account balance is over $5,000, you can leave the money in your old company retirement plan. Another option is to pay the income tax on the rollover and check to see if you qualify for a Roth IRA.

Never take the money and run.

After federal and possible state income taxes, and a 10 percent early withdrawal penalty under the age of 59 ½, taking the money could cost you a fortune at retirement age.

But, according to Fidelity Investments 40 percent of Gen X and Gen Y – 20- to 40 year olds cashed out their 401(k) money when they changed jobs.

Burn this difference into your mind
You are 40, have 25 years to Social Security:

Let's say the rollover is $25,000.

Take the cash and run:		**$25,000**
Less income taxes 25%		**18,750**
Less 10% withdrawal fee 2,500		**16,250**

Under this example you have to fork over $8,750, leaving you just $16,250 to spend. You can, of course, run wild at the shopping mall. But let's see what could happen had you rolled the entire $25,000 tax free into an IRA and make no further contributions.

At age 40, one time deposit of $25,000
At age 65, the IRA could be worth $270,000

I can think of no better way to explain the importance of rolling over the money into an IRA than the difference of taking $16,250 to a shopping mall, or spending $270,000 in retirement.

The company matching dance

Another major task for most workers is how to take advantage of the employer's matching contributions. The first step is to determine the monthly payroll deduction you need to earn the employer's maximum matching dollars. Don't be the typical worker who leaves the company money on the table and not in their retirement plan.

Here's why. Hewitt Associates, a big employee benefit firm, found that only half the retirement plan participants divert 3 percent of pay. And 28 percent put in just 2 percent of pay. At many companies that's not enough to qualify for the matching program.

Right now is a good time to check on how much payroll deduction [as a percentage of your salary] is required to qualify for the maximum company match. The higher payroll deduction – even if it's only a few dollars a month more - could make a huge difference in grabbing the company's match money and the value of your future retirement nest egg.

Here's how this could work:

If your salary is $60,000, a 3 percent salary

deduction of $150 a month might create an employers match of 50 cents on the dollar. Your annual contribution of $1,800 would be matched by $900, or a total of $2,700. In three years, this could amount to $9,860, of which you contributed only $5,400.

A 6 percent salary deduction of $300 a month might be matched dollar for dollar. Your annual contribution of $3,600 could be matched by $3,600, or a total of $7,200. In 3 years this could amount to $26,000, of which you would have contributed only $10,800.

Even if you look at the numbers through blood shot eyes you can see in this last example you contributed $3,600 a year from your pay and the retirement account grew, on average, by $8,600 each year. Not bad: $10,800 out of your paycheck and $26,000 in the retirement account.

But the scary part, if you remember the lessons on compounding, is with 6 percent of salary into matching contributions for just 7 more years – a total of 10 years – you would have contributed $36,000 and your retirement account could be worth $126,000.

Again, if you divide the $126,000 by 10 years, the average annual increase in the retirement account is $12,600 with an annual contribution of just $3,600. Believe me; earning these numbers over a longer period of time can make you rich!

A final thought

As I talk with people who read the early copies of this book I learned they had found the courage to do the 15-minute drills each week. As the new way to invest became more familiar they moved from newspapers to bigcharts.com and then to online IRA accounts which automatically displayed their stocks and funds.

As they gained more confidence in managing their money, they realized that what once held them in fear of the unknown was not as terrible as they had imagined. Now, they tell me, they feel on top of their game because they know whatever they save and invest each month, compounding could multiply that by as much as 9 or 10 times when they retire.

Maybe you don't think this plan will work for you. But Trend Investing and compounding has worked for professional investors, those I met working on Wall Street and those callers on my WOR radio program in New York and KGO in San Francisco, and there's no reason to think it won't work for you.

Remember, if you believe in the power of change, you can change the way you invest your money. And if you start right now, like thousands of other people who have built sizeable retirement nest eggs at all ages, you'll find this change can lead you to a new and better financial life.

Most important of all, make up your mind that you're going to learn the basic keys to building wealth and then manage your own money. I hope you find your dream of financial independence. I know you have every opportunity to do so.

Next, take these steps now

To build a hefty retirement nest egg you need to save for retirement with an absolute order of priority:

First, make payroll deductions into the employer's plan to trigger the maximum company match program. If your company does not have a matching program, sign up for payroll deductions into your own individual retirement account.

Second: Open your IRA and make as much of the allowable contributions as you can. Remember, a working spouse at home without taxable income can also participate in an IRA on the same basis as the employed spouse.

Third: Remember the side bet: Find out how you can add to your IRA or other personal savings account on a monthly basis. Sure, you don't have to make the IRA contributions until April 15 of the following year, or until you file your income taxes, but if you get in the habit of contributing in January of the previous year you'll benefit from the additional 15 months of appreciation. Assuming you add $4,000 a year to your IRA at the start of the year you'll have earned about $26,000 in five years, only $18,000 by making the contribution just before tax time."

Fourth: Keep track of each investment with the 15-minute rule each weekend. As we've seen in the stock market meltdown of 2009, knowing when to sell is as important as knowing when to buy.

Now What?

First: Read this little book again. Maybe at least once a month as you put into play the many ideas that can build a solid retirement income.

Second: Share copies of the book with the important people in your life so you can discuss the many ways you can sell as the stock starts to turn down and buy again once the price of the stock turns up.

Third: Go to the end of this book and order a free trial subscription to Jim Jorgensen's weekly e-newsletter with the latest news on managing your money and saving for retirement. In each internet newsletter is segments of his radio program that allows you to listen and read the important investment and retirement topics of the day.

About The Author

Jim Jorgensen has over thirty years' experience in financial planning, as a broker on Wall Street and an investment consultant. He is the author of seven books on personal finance, including **The Graying of America**. His last book was **It's Never Too Late To Get Rich**, published by Simon & Schuster.

He has been a radio host on WOR in New York City and ABC and CBS in San Francisco. For over the past decade he has been host of **Jorgensen On Money,** a syndicated radio show which can be heard on the internet, downloaded to an I Pod or other listening devices, and on major financial web sites.

Jim is a frequent speaker at conventions and meetings and brings his down-to-earth study of investing on Wall Street and economic forecast to audiences worldwide. He provides employees with information on their company retirement plans, and his clients often video his talk for employees in other locations.

He writes, with his son Richard Jorgensen, who covers technology from Silicon Valley, a weekly electronic **Financial Savvy Report** which lands on subscribes desks each Monday. For his clients he also manages money based on what he learns from his early days on Wall Street.

He and his wife Nancy reside near Palm Springs California.

Thank you for reading this book!

To keep you up to date on the latest ways to manage your money with Trend Investing and build your 401(k), IRA and Roth IRA, Jim Jorgensen wants you to receive a no-risk 3-week **free trial subscription** to his e-newsletter:

The Financial Savvy Repot

Your buyer's code is 4379

Each week in the on-line report you'll read the latest inside market investment and retirement news and listen to segments of Jim's radio program imbedded in the Report.

To receive your free trial subscription, send an e-mail to Info@financialsavvy.com, with your name, address, buyer's code and your comments on the book. In the subject line use your code 4379.

To book Jim Jorgensen as your next keynote speaker, his website is: **www.JimJorgensen.com** or call 1-800-558-4558.

Here Did My Money Go?

Share it with others...

This book is also available at special quantity discounts for bulk purchases for sales promotions, premiums, fund-raising, or educational use. The books can be created to fit special needs. Call 1-800-558-4558 or e-mail info@financialsavvy.com for more information.